JAZZ DRUMSET SOLOS

7 CONTEMPORARY PIECES by Sperie Karas

ISBN 978-0-634-06549-1

HAL•LEONARD®
CORPORATION

7777 W. BLUEMOUND RD. P.O. BOX 13819 MILWAUKEE, WI 53213

In Australia Contact:
Hal Leonard Australia Pty. Ltd.
22 Taunton Drive P.O. Box 5130
Cheltenham East, 3192 Victoria, Australia
Email: ausadmin@halleonard.com

CONTENTS

FEEL THE JAZZ
Solo for Drumset

By Sperie Karas

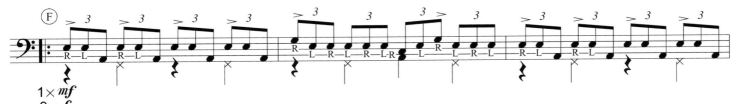

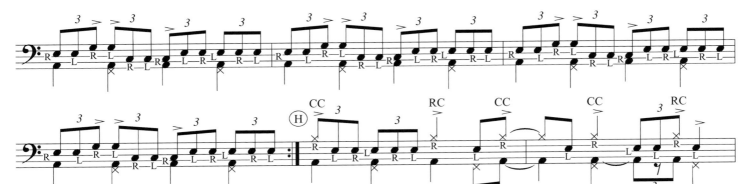

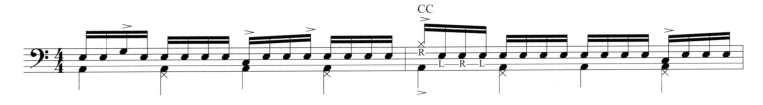

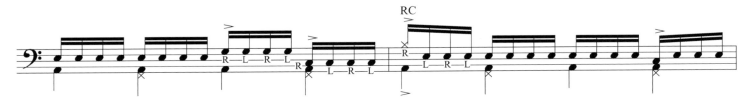

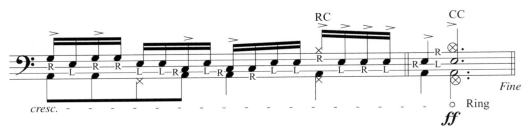

KEY

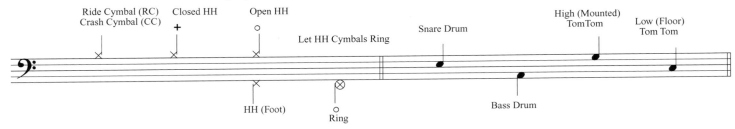

UPTOWN WALTZ
Solo for Drumset

By Sperie Karas

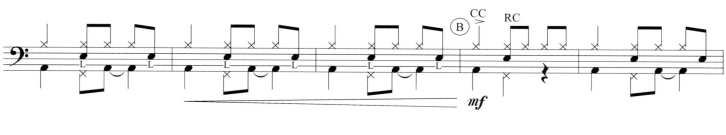

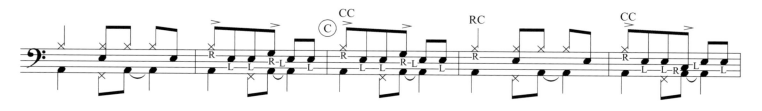

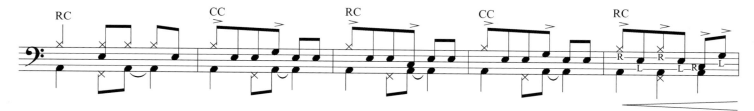

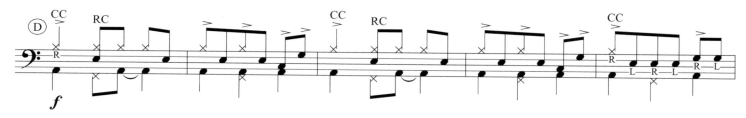

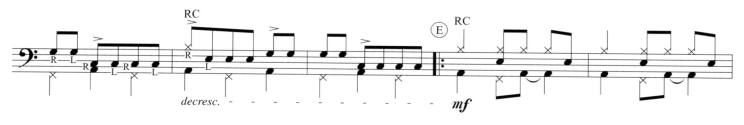

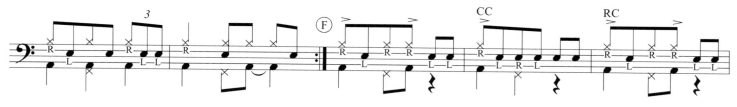

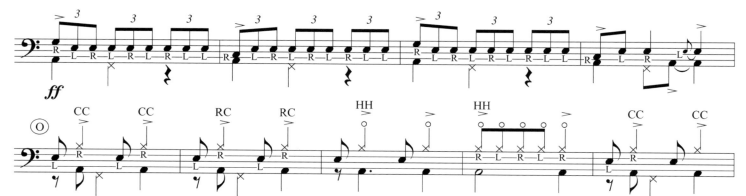

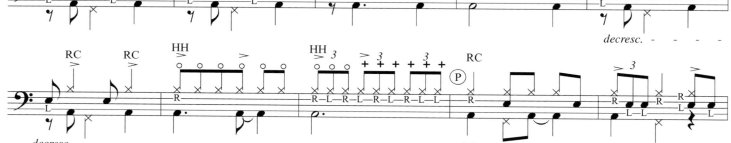

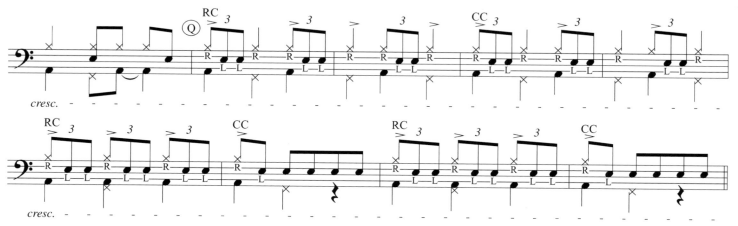

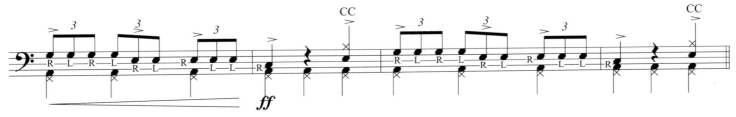

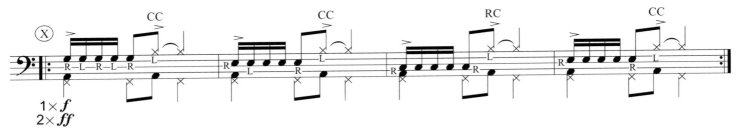

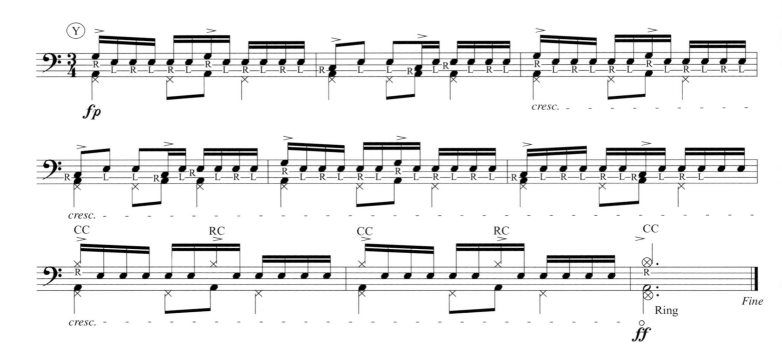

KEY

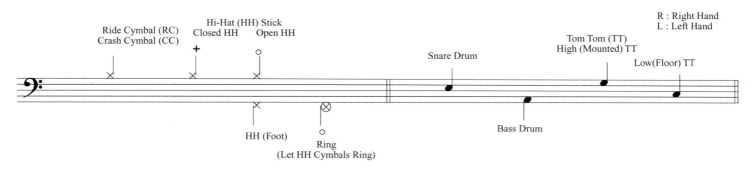

BRUSH FIRE
Solo for Drumset with Brushes

Med. Fast Jazz ♩♩ = ♩³♩

♩ = ca. 146

By Sperie Karas

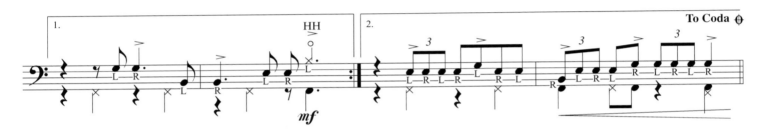

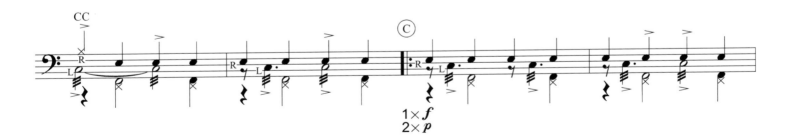

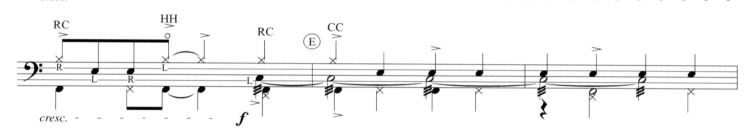

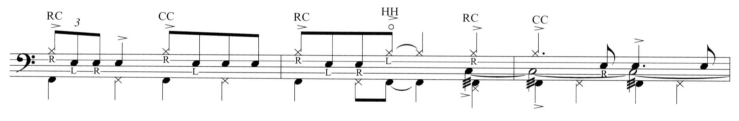

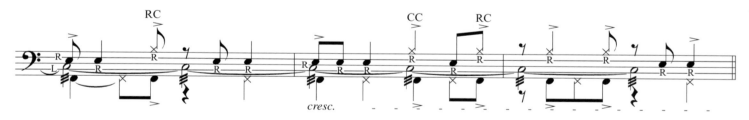

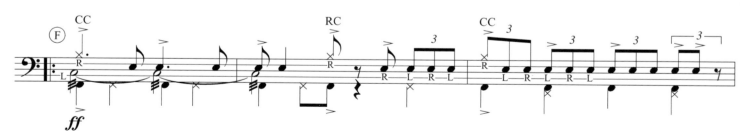

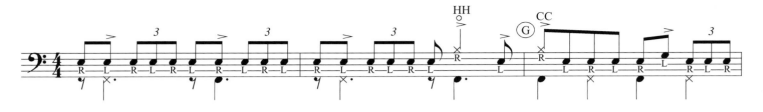

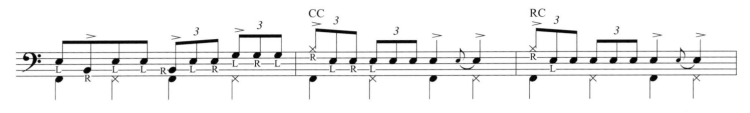

D.C. al Coda
(with repeats)

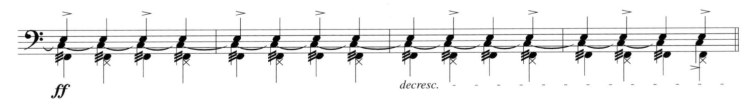

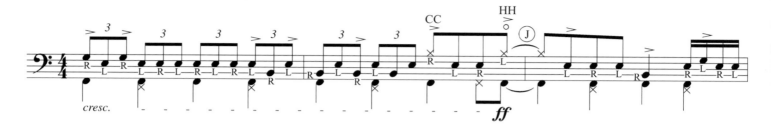

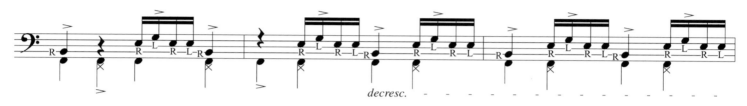

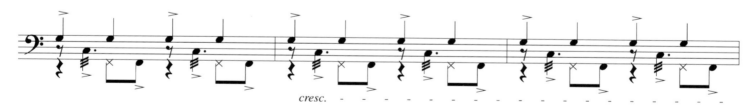

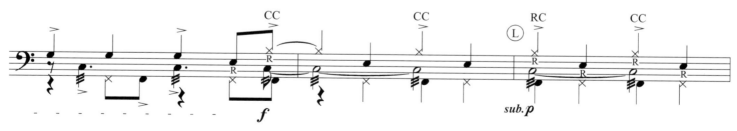

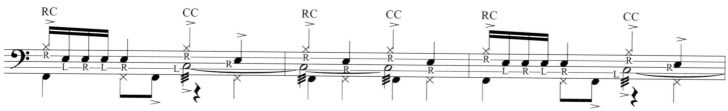

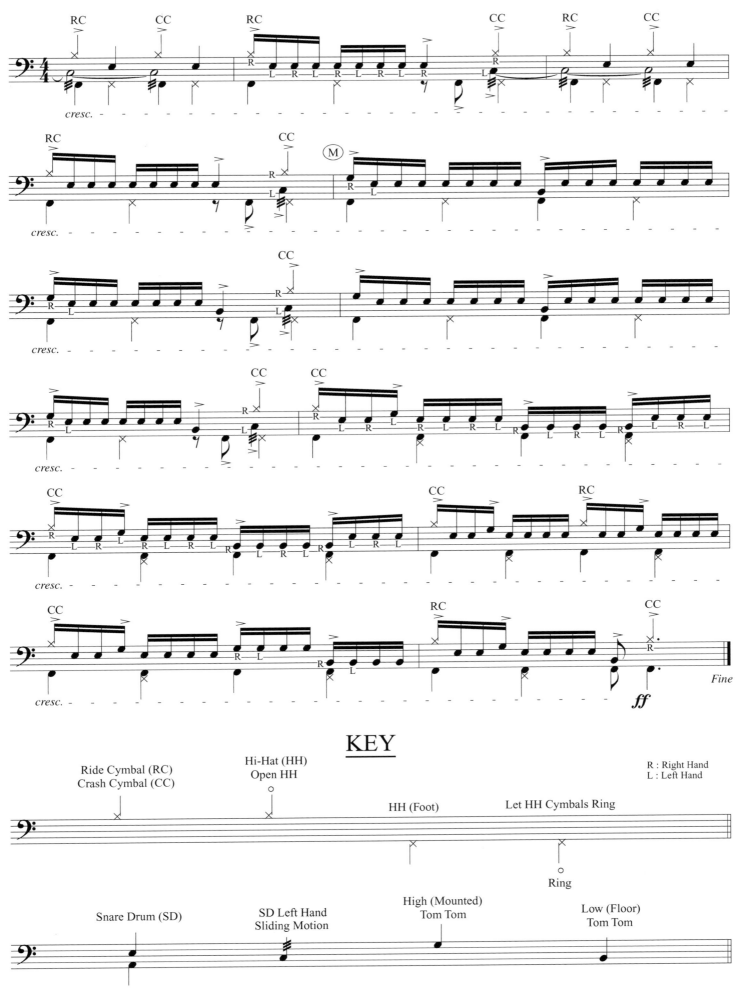

KEY

VOYAGE EAST
Solo for Drumset

By Sperie Karas

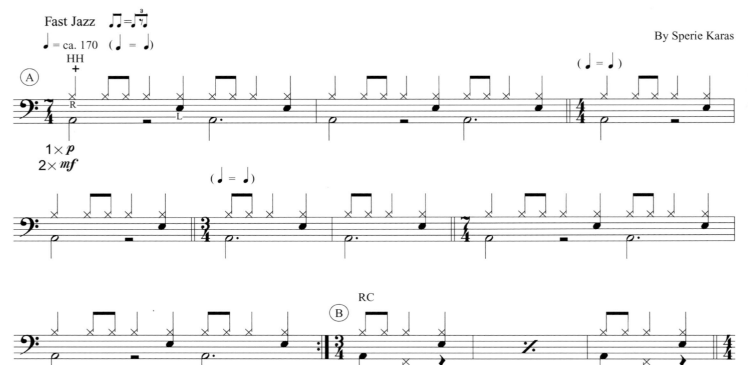

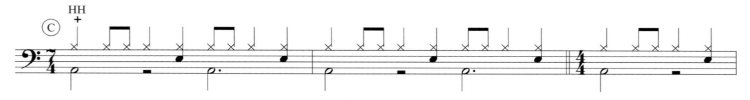

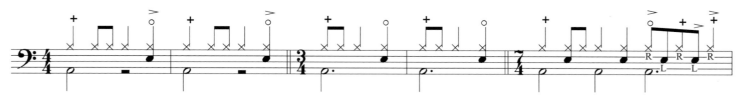

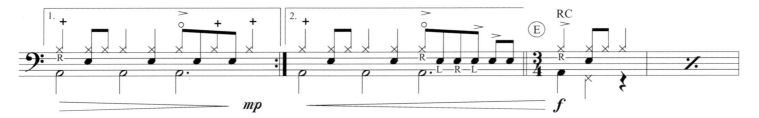

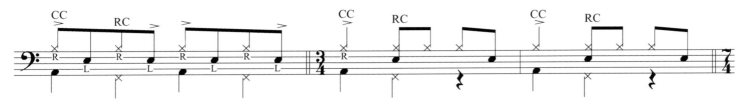

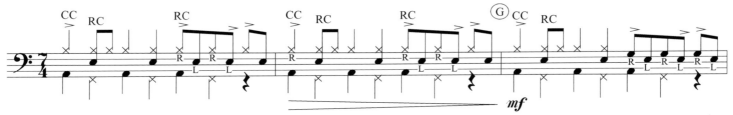

KEY

FIVE'S THE TIME
Solo for Drumset

By Sperie Karas

24

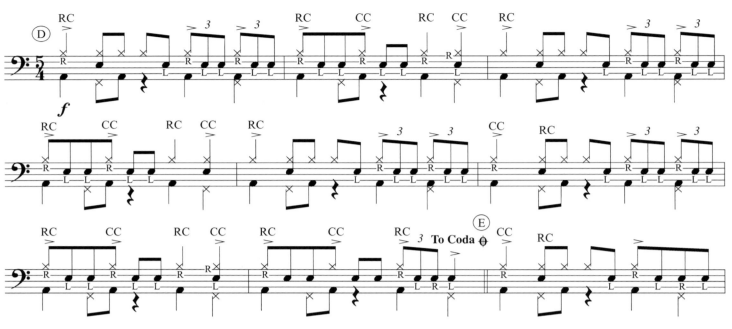

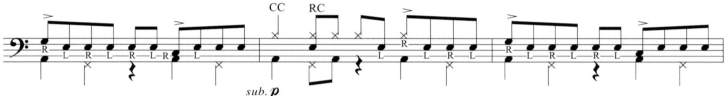

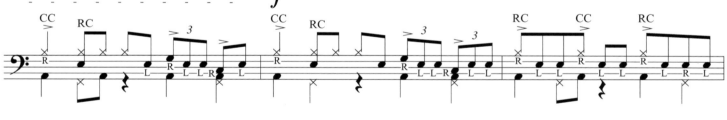

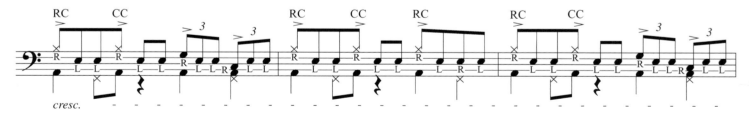

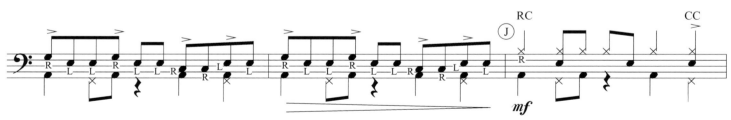

25

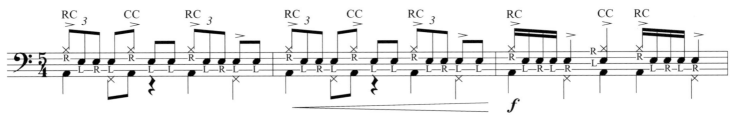

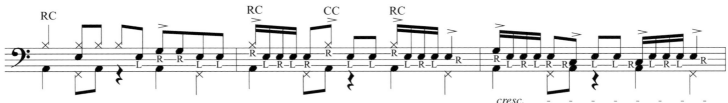

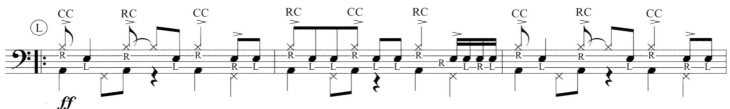

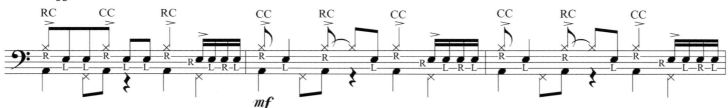

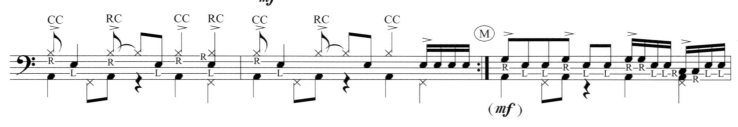

KEY

LATIN FANTASY
Solo for Drumset

By Sperie Karas

Fast Latin

♩ = ca. 86

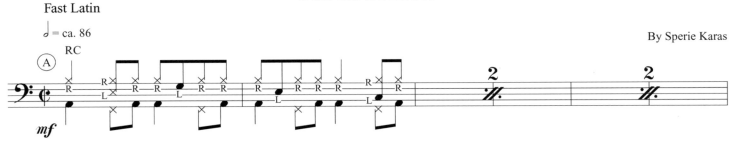

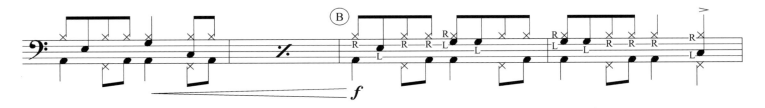

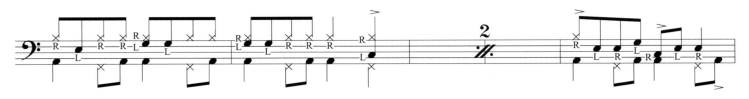

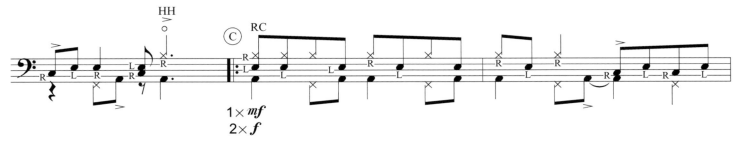

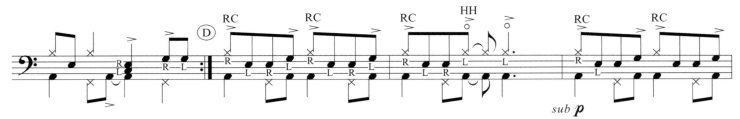

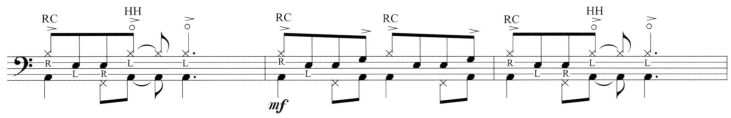

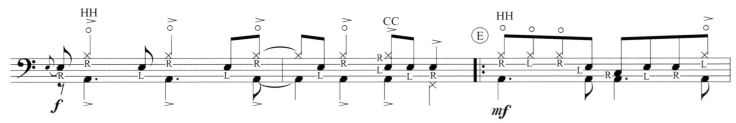

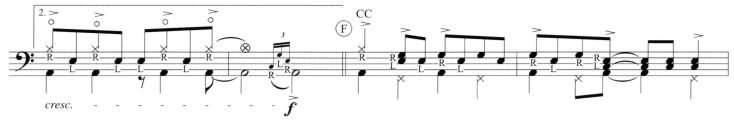

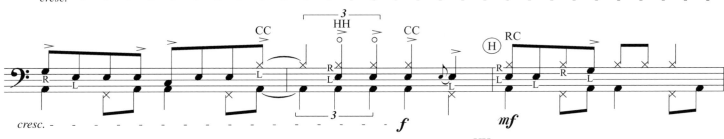

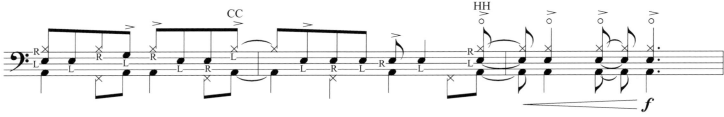

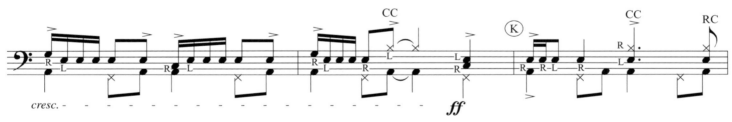

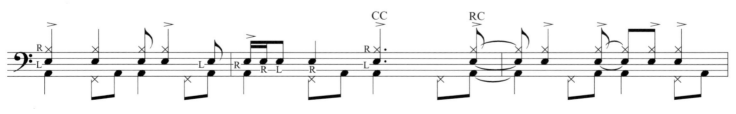

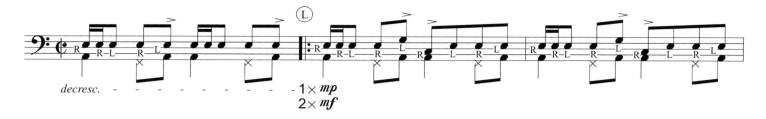

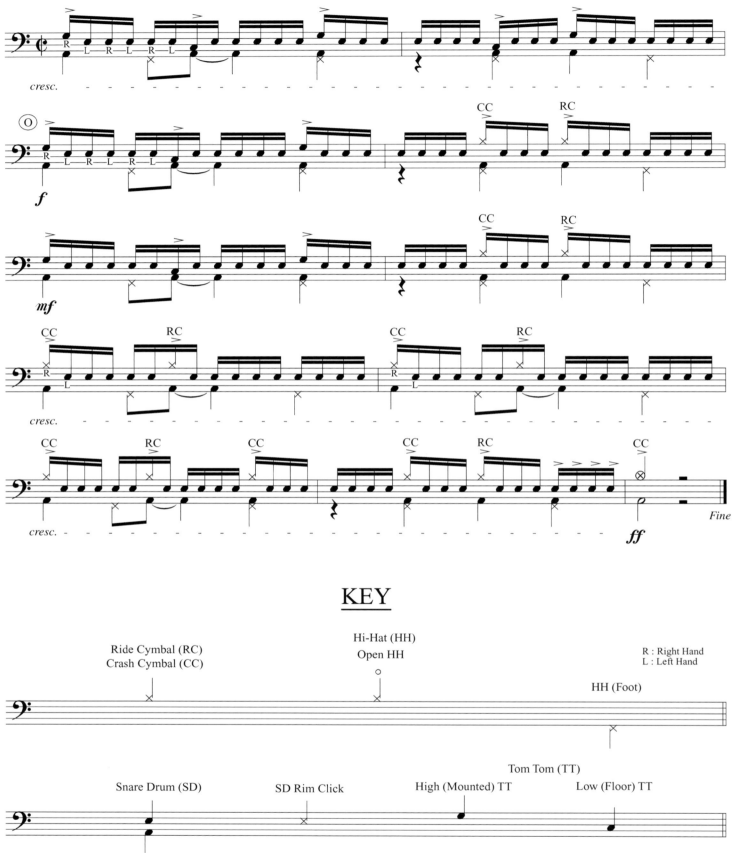

KEY

ROAR
Solo for drumset

By Sperie Karas

Fast Jazz

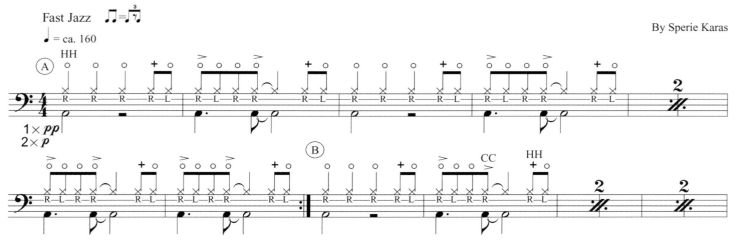

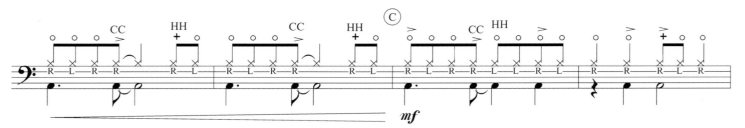

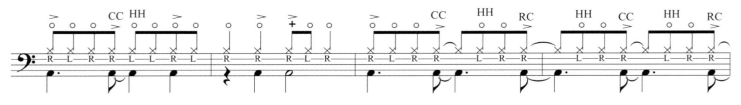

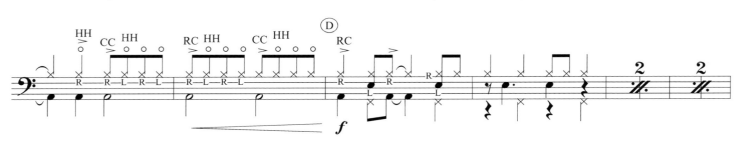

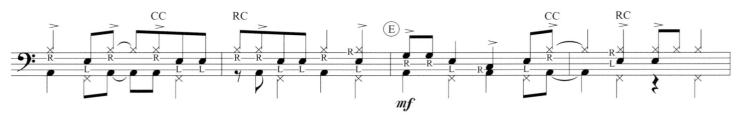

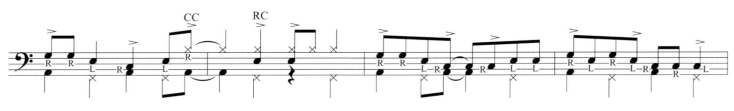

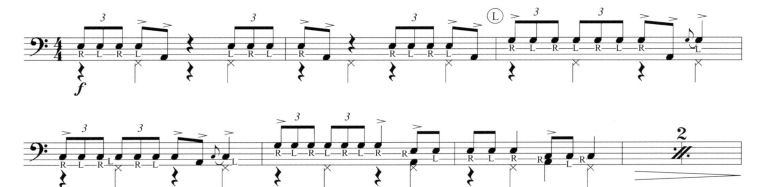

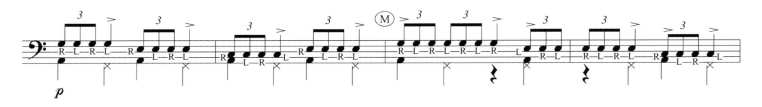

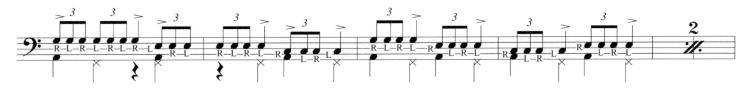

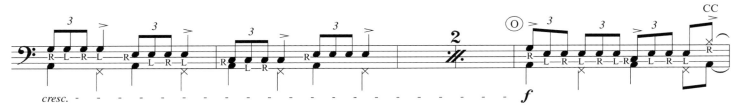

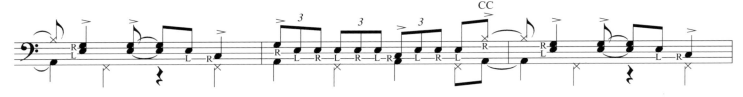

YOU CAN'T BEAT OUR DRUM BOOKS!